A Monarch Butterfly's Journey

by Suzanne Slade

illustrated by Susan Swan

PICTURE WINDOW BOOKS

a capstone imprint

Thanks to our advisers for their expertise, research, and advice:

Jerald Dosch, PhD
Director, Katharine Ordway Natural History Study Area
Visiting Assistant Professor of Biology
Macalester College

Terry Flaherty, PhD
Professor of English
Minnesota State University, Mankato

Editor: Jill Kalz
Designer: Tracy Davies
Art Director: Nathan Gassman
Production Specialist: Sarah Bennett
The illustrations in this book were created with mixed media/found object.

Picture Window Books
151 Good Counsel Drive
P.O. Box 669
Mankato, MN 56002-0669
877-845-8392
www.capstonepub.com

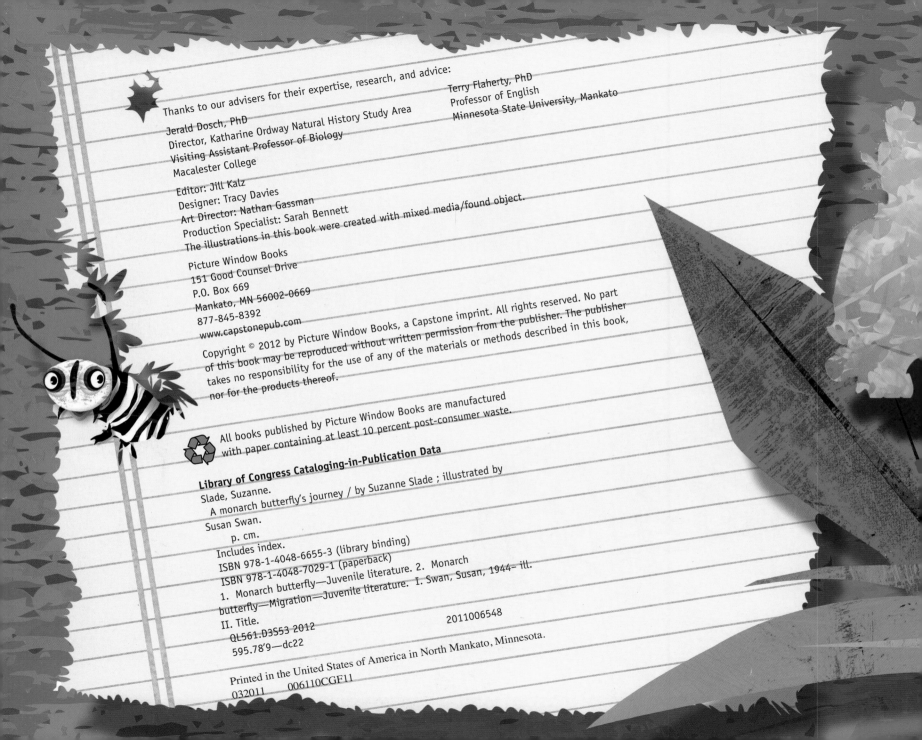

All books published by Picture Window Books are manufactured with paper containing at least 10 percent post-consumer waste.

Library of Congress Cataloging-in-Publication Data
Slade, Suzanne.
   A monarch butterfly's journey / by Suzanne Slade ; illustrated by Susan Swan.
      p. cm.
   Includes index.
   ISBN 978-1-4048-6655-3 (library binding)
   ISBN 978-1-4048-7029-1 (paperback)
   1. Monarch butterfly—Juvenile literature. 2. Monarch butterfly—Migration—Juvenile literature. I. Swan, Susan, 1944– ill.
II. Title.
   QL561.D3S53 2012
   595.78′9—dc22
                                                    2011006548

Printed in the United States of America in North Mankato, Minnesota.
032011   006110CGF11

Look closely.

Something very small and special is hiding on this milkweed plant. Below pink flowers and thick green leaves sits a tiny white spot.

An egg!

I may be small, but I have big plans!

3

Suddenly, the egg begins to wiggle. A tiny larva crawls out of the top. It's a monarch caterpillar. And it's about to go on a long journey with a long name: *metamorphosis*.

The caterpillar's first job? Eating! It dines on its eggshell. Then it munches the juicy milkweed leaves.

I am a munching machine!

Monarch caterpillars eat only one kind of leaf: milkweed. Milkweed leaves have a special chemical in them that protects the caterpillars from being eaten. The chemical makes the caterpillars taste bad. It also makes them poisonous.

The monarch caterpillar eats day and night.

CRUNCH. CRUNCH.

I LOVE all-you-can-eat buffets!

Soon the caterpillar outgrows its skin.

When the old skin comes off, a new skin is already underneath. The hungry caterpillar eats and grows, eats and grows.

After shedding four times in two weeks, the caterpillar is ready for a big change.

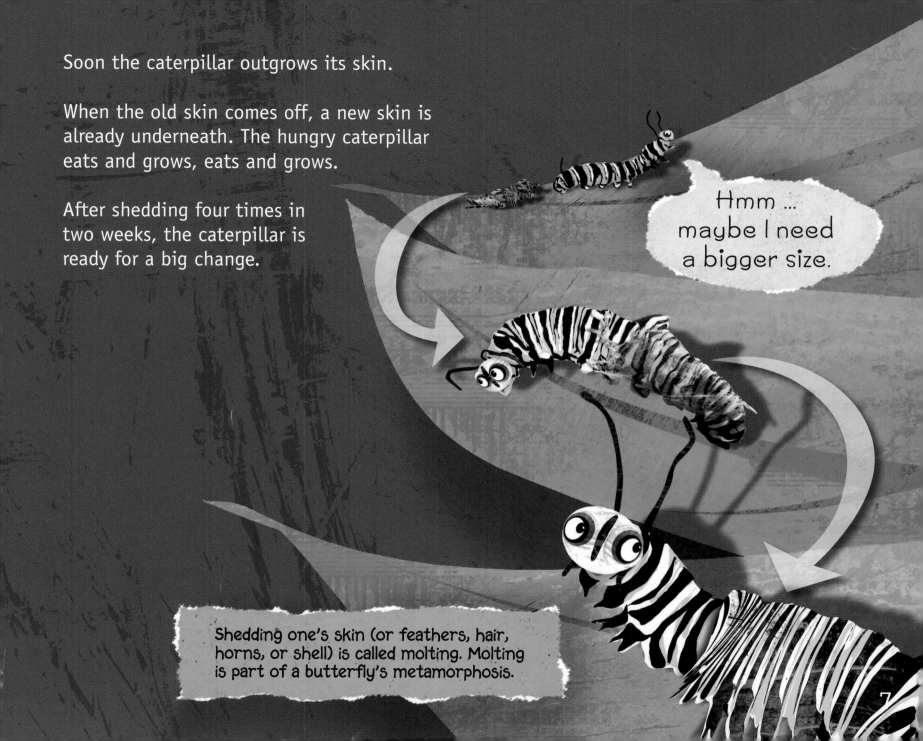

Hmm ... maybe I need a bigger size.

Shedding one's skin (or feathers, hair, horns, or shell) is called molting. Molting is part of a butterfly's metamorphosis.

7

Using silk thread, the monarch caterpillar attaches its back end to a branch. It curls into a J. Then it jerks back and forth and sheds one last time.

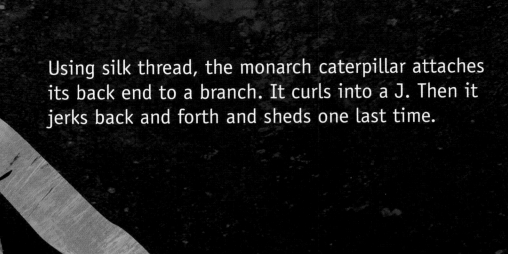

The outer layer hardens and forms a chrysalis. The chrysalis sparkles like a jewel. And the caterpillar? It's now a pupa!

GRAND OPENING in 10-14 days!

The chrysalis hangs still and quiet. The green shell turns clear. Black and orange stripes appear inside.

This is a nice place to hang.

9

After about nine days, the chrysalis darkens. Then,

CRACK!– out crawls a creature with wet, wrinkled wings.

A monarch butterfly!

Awesome! I can't wait to try my new wings!

After drying its wings, the butterfly flutters from flower to flower. It drinks nectar and stores energy for the long journey ahead.

A monarch butterfly has a few jobs to do before its first flight. First, it pumps up its wings. Then it dries them in the sun and wind. Finally, it must fix together the two pieces of its proboscis. The butterfly needs this long tube for feeding.

When the cool, short days of fall arrive, the monarch butterfly heads south with thousands of other monarchs. The northern winter is too cold for them. They fly over small towns and grand cities.

Along the way, more monarch butterflies join the migration. They stop to rest and drink nectar near rivers, ponds, and fields. They use the nectar to fuel their flight. But they also store some of it as fat. The butterflies will live off this fat all winter.

What a workout!

Try a sip of this!

WHOOSH! WHOOSH! WHOOSH!

Countless flapping wings echo through the warm air. They sound like rushing water.

I love Mexico!

As the sun sinks in the sky, the butterfly looks for a place to rest. It finds a large cluster of butterflies in a tall fir tree and cuddles close to stay warm. Millions of monarchs settle in for the night.

16

Each fall, millions of monarch butterflies migrate to Mexico. They spend the winter there. They come from the northern and eastern parts of the United States and southern Canada. Monarchs from western states migrate to California.

Snug in the sunny Mexican forest, the monarch butterfly rests all winter long. It may go days without moving at all. On warm afternoons it stretches its wings and searches for food.

When March arrives, the butterfly gets ready to fly back north. It searches for a partner and mates.

The monarch butterfly flutters out of Mexico and glides across wide, windy skies. As it travels, it leaves behind something very small and special—eggs. The butterfly lays hundreds of eggs on milkweed plants.

Each generation of butterflies lives only six to eight weeks. These new butterflies continue flying north and laying eggs before they die. The last group of eggs, which hatches in August and September, is different. This generation lives about eight months and makes the long flight to Mexico in fall.

This is where the butterfly's journey ends. But soon the eggs will hatch and fill the sky with brand-new monarch butterflies!

You'll be a fine flier someday!

Diagram of a Monarch Butterfly's Journey

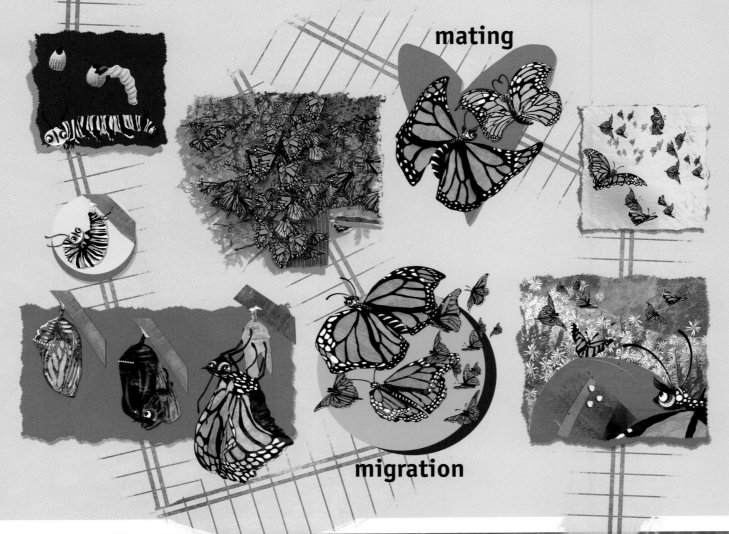

egg

mating

migration

Glossary

chrysalis—the hard shell inside which a pupa changes into a butterfly

larva—an animal in the stage of growth between egg and pupa

mate—to join together to produce young

metamorphosis—the series of changes some animals go through as they grow from eggs to adults

migration—the movement from one place to another, often to find food

nectar—a sweet liquid formed inside flowers

pupa—an animal in the stage of growth between larva and adult

silk—a thin, strong thread made by some insects

To Learn More

More Books to Read

Frost, Helen, and Leonid Gore. *Monarch and Milkweed.* New York: Atheneum Books for Young Readers, 2008.

Kelly, Irene. *It's a Butterfly's Life.* New York: Holiday House, 2007.

Slade, Suzanne. *From Caterpillar to Butterfly: Following the Life Cycle.* Amazing Science. Life Cycles. Minneapolis: Picture Window Books, 2009.

Internet Sites

FactHound offers a safe, fun way to find Internet sites related to this book. All of the sites on FactHound have been researched by our staff.

Here's all you do:
Visit *www.facthound.com*
Type in this code: 9781404866553

Super-cool stuff!

Check out projects, games and lots more at
www.capstonekids.com

Index

California, 17
caterpillars, 4, 5, 6–7
chrysalises, 8–10
eating, 5, 6, 7, 11, 14
eggs, 3, 4, 5, 20, 21
larvae, 4
leaves, 3, 5
mating, 19
metamorphosis, 4, 7
Mexico, 17, 18, 20
migration, 12, 13, 14, 17

milkweed, 3, 5, 20
molting, 7, 8
proboscis, 11
pupae, 8
shedding. *See* molting
skin, 7
wings, 10, 11, 16, 18

Look for all the books in the Follow It series:

A Bill's Journey into Law

A Dollar Bill's Journey

A Germ's Journey

A Monarch Butterfly's Journey

A Plastic Bottle's Journey

A Raindrop's Journey